IF

I

WERE

IN

CHARGE

THE

RULES

WOULD

BE

DIFFERENT

Poems and drawings by James Proimos

SCHOLASTIC INC.
New York Toronto London Auckland Sydney
Mexico City New Delhi Hong Kong Buenos Aires

IF

I

WERE

IN

CHARGE

THE

RULES

WOULD

BE

DIFFERENT

ISBN 0-439-20865-3

12 11 10 9 8 7 6 5 4 3 2 1   2 3 4 5 6 7/0

Printed in the U.S.A.   40

First Scholastic paperback printing,
September 2002

The art in this book was created with a Sharpie on paper, scanned, and then colored on an iMac in Adobe Photoshop LE.

This book was set in Kosmik-PlainOne
Book design by Yvette Awad

this

book,

like

the

rest

of

my

life,

is

dedicated

to

jolie

I'm Sitting Here at the Bus Stop

Will one come now?
Will one come soon?
While I wait
I hum a tune.

I brought a sandwich
tuna on rye.
Food really helps
to make the time go by.

People ask me,
"When's the next bus due?"
I tell them I don't know
and that I'm waiting, too.

But I'm not waiting for a bus.
I'm just one block from home.
This bench is a perfect place to sit
when waiting for a poem.

Hey! What's that ruckus down the road?
It looks like poems! A whole truckload!
Big enough to fill a book.
Wait here while I write them down
then peek inside and have a look.

BUS STOP

The One-Ton Pooch

I have a 2,000-pound pooch,
which is pretty super dooper.
The only part that I don't like
involves his giant pooper scooper.

My Feet Stink. Does Your Nose Smell?

My feet stink.
Does your nose smell?
Because
if it doesn't,
we'll get along swell.

My feet stink.
Smell them, will you?
Wait!
You'd better not—
the stench might kill you.

My feet stink.
May I smell yours?
Hey!
Those smell nice,
may I smell some more?

SNIFF
SNIFF

The Late Show

I stayed up till midnight
and I'm as awake as I can be.
My parents said I'd be tired today
but they—Zzzzzzzzzzzzzzz

If I Were in Charge the Rules Would Be Different

It hurts me to lecture you, Mommy,
but you didn't eat all your salami.
Plus, your room is way too neat
and you have socks on both your feet.
Why in the world, may I ask,
did you go and take out the trash?
You also get every inch of blame
for hardly playing your video game.
Oh, after all you put me through,
what am I gonna do with you?
Go to your room and don't come out
until you learn to whine and pout!

A PHOTO OF A UFO OR YOUR GRANDPA'S CIGAR?

BIG FOOT'S TOE OR YOUR UNCLE LARRY'S?

THE LOCH NESS MONSTER OR A CLOSE-UP OF TOOTIE, YOUR GOLDFISH?

The Search of the Century

UFOs are one thing
and Bigfoot is another.
You want to look for the Loch Ness monster?
Why would you even bother?

Everyone's already seen E.T.
and Bigfoot is passé.
What's so great about a giant sea serpent?
People catch fish every day.

I say, "Why go all the way to the moon
just to bring back rocks?"
I'd travel the entire universe
to find just one of my missing socks.

General Mary Rumpus Addresses the Troops

Vegetables are the enemy.
We must do all we can to beat them.
Unfortunately, the only way to win the war
is to pick up your fork and eat them.

Ode to Spaghetti

Spaghetti, I salute you.
I love you oodles and oodles.
You deserve a major award
for being champ of the noodles.

I'M NOT WORTHY.

I Want My Mommy

I want my mommy,
nothing against yours.
But my mommy is so magnificent
I'm thinking of giving tours.

I want my mommy,
she's the cream of the crop, you know.
She's the Cadillac of mommies.
She's the Best of Best of Show.

I want my mommy,
and you can keep your mother.
Of course, if you come up with the right deal,
you can have my baby brother.

The Slide

I got on this slide after breakfast
and I've been stuck halfway down since noon.
If someone could give me a push,
I might reach the ground by June.

I See a Lot of Me in My Daddy

I see a lot of me in my daddy,

especially when I jump into his bed,

and I snuggle up real close,

and see my reflection in his

big

bald

head.

Rethinking Baths

You hate baths? Ha!
What a funny fellow!
I'll assume you've never taken one
in a tub of Jell-O.

Billy Snudlang

When Billy Snudlang
picks a team,
I am the last one chose.

Of course,

If Billy Snudlang
only got one pick,
he would pick his nose.

Trash Talk

I don't like taking out the trash,
I don't like folding clothes.
I don't like washing dishes,
or shoveling when it snows.

What I do like is doing nothing,
lying flat on my back,
watching some bad TV show,
while eating a nice snack.

Yeah, I've let things pile up—
the snow, the dishes, the clothes, the trash.
But I wouldn't live my life differently
for any amount of cash.

You may say I'm lazy
or think that I'm a bore,
I won't be by to defend myself
because I can't get out my door.

Isn't Nature Wonderful?

I once ate a caterpillar,
it's no lie.
Yesterday I burped—
out came a butterfly.

My Grandma's Like a Thermos

A thermos knows when to keep things hot
and when to keep things cold.
Even before you ask it,
it does what it is told.

It's kind of like Grandma,
who knows exactly what to say,
even before I tell her I'm happy,
or that I'm having a mushy sort of day.

THERMOS   GRANDMA

Kid Restaurant

Welcome to my restaurant!
I created it for kids like you.
Nothing is dull or boring or average
or exceptionally hard to chew.

Would you like some delicious tree bark?
It's topped with blades of grass,
and covered in a wonderful gravy
made of worms that I have mashed!

Maybe you should start with an appetizer?
Today's special is bumblebee wings.
They're made with a special hot sauce.
Please avoid the part that stings.

For dessert I recommend the pudding,
which gets its smoothness from pureed flies.
But you'll especially like the lumpy bits,
culled from the corners of my eyes.

It's the best kind of food in the universe,
though I admit business has been slow.
So what would you like to order?
Hey! Where did you go?

Homework
Tip

Whenever you do your homework
pretend you're on a plane,
that makes it more like vacationwork
and it's harder to complain.

Don't Mess With Mom

"Go ahead,
make
my
day,"
to my mother I willfully said.
"Hey, wise guy," she replied in turn.
"Go ahead
and
make
your
bed."

Lola, the Singing Octopus

I'm in love with Lola the Octopus
and the angelic way that she sings.
Oh, how I wish I could marry her
but who can afford eight rings?

The Monster

I'm trying to sleep
but there's a monster in the next room.
He almost got me once
but I fought him off with a broom.
He did seriously mangle one of my dollies
and he ripped off the head of another.
He's mean and he's ugly and he's bad and no good.
Worst of all he's my little brother.

Ode to a Peanut Butter and Jelly Sandwich

Thank you, Mr. Peanut Butter.
Thank you, Mrs. Jelly.
Thank you from all of me,
especially from my belly!

The Singer

My sister loves to sing.
She'll sing about anything.
She'll sing about babies,
mashed potatoes and gravy.
She'll sing about cooties
or ten bathing beauties.
She'll sing about love,
a push or a shove.
She'll even sing about a rock
or a missing left sock.
But what makes me mad as mad can be
is that she doesn't ever sing about me!

Paul Carolina Flushed Himself to China

On a very sunny day
in sunny ol' L.A.
Paul Carolina
flushed himself to China
where he met a lady flossing her teeth
who promptly flushed him over to Greece.
There a plumber draining a drain
turned and flushed Paul directly to Spain
where a girl who was combing her long silky hair
daintily flushed him to Delaware.
A man there had a few nasty words to say
before flushing Paul back to sunny L.A.
So although it was not his original goal
Paul saw the world from his toilet bowl.

Little Help

Hello, I'm your belly button.
This is the first poem I ever wrote.
I would've told you verbally,
but I have no vocal cords or throat.

I hate to write so bluntly,
but there's no time left to hint.
You have to lend a hand down here,
and pick out all this lint!

OH MY!

Fashion Critic

I've worn all kinds of clothes
from extremely elegant to the casually crude,
but when it comes right down to it,
I much prefer being nude.

Love (Yuck) Poem

If you were falling down a cliff,
way above the land,
and if you reached out to me,
yeah, sure, I'd hold your hand.

I generally don't write love poems.
It's just not what I do.
But something came over me today,
and I wrote this poem for you.

If a poisonous snake bit your nose,
right on its bulbous base,
and if it meant you wouldn't die,
yeah, sure, I'd suck your face.

I generally don't write love poems.
It's just not what I do.
But something came over me today,
and I wrote this poem for you.

My Best Friend

Maximilian Luther McCree
must have a brain the size of a pea.
He can't add one plus three
or even recite the alphabet to C.
But he's the best friend that could ever be
and that's more than good enough for me.

A Poem About My Uncle Larry (Who Never Wore a Suit) and His Wedding

My Uncle Larry was told he had to wear a suit,
if he didn't mind
(but he did).
So, he showed up at his wedding
in the bathing kind.

The
Hat
Stays

I'm never taking off this hat
and there's nothing you can do.
You couldn't get it off me
with a wrecking crew.

You could pay me a million bucks
and I wouldn't remove this derby.
It makes me feel like a movie star
and hugs my head superbly.

This hat stays right where it is, all right.
I won't remove a stitch.
I'm gonna leave it on for a kajillion years—
starting right after I scratch this itch.

Don't Hate Me Because I'm the Teacher's Pet

Hey, I don't wildly raise my hand all the time,
or bring her an apple each day.
I don't remind her to give us homework,
or report the bad things you say.

Then how did I get to be the teacher's pet?
Well, it happened yesterday at two-thirtyish.
She walked directly into the store,
and said, "I'll take that fish!"

Ode to Asparagus

Asparagus, you are mighty.
You're wonderfully fantastic.
You're fifty times better than Raspberry Fudge Swirl.
Can you tell that I'm sarcastic?

The Best
Fans in
Baseball

They threw me out at third.
That's how we lost the game.
I couldn't keep from crying
because I'm the guy they blame.

The team won't speak to me.
The coach said far too much.
And that girl I gave my number to
won't likely be in touch.

But my dad gave me a hug,
and my mom wrote me a poem.
Yeah, they threw me out at third
but now I'm safe at home.

The True Story of How I Blew a Bubble as Big as My Head

When I was only seven,
while lying in my bed,
I put a wad of gum in my mouth
and blew a bubble as big as my head.

When my father told my mother,
"Heavens to Betsy!" was what she said.
"A son of ours is talented enough
to blow a bubble as big as his head!"

They gathered all my siblings,
Arthur, Mary, Walter, and Ted.
"Who else here is wonderful enough
to blow a bubble as big as their head!"

When *The New York Times* did the story,
the gigantic headline read:
FORGET THE HURRICANE,
EARTHQUAKE, AND STOCK MARKET CRASH—
SOME KID BLEW A BUBBLE AS BIG AS HIS HEAD!

I was invited to dine with the president
where I was neither lied to nor misled.
He pinned me with the nation's greatest honor,
the medal for blowing a bubble as big as your head.

Last week a kid blew a bubble as big as a Buick,
and now she's the star instead.
But I'll never forget that glorious moment
I blew a bubble as big as my head.

BOY BLOWS BUBBLE AS BIG AS HIS HEAD! NEWS AT 11:00!
NEWS ALERT! NEWS ALERT! NE

Friends

My pony is my best friend.
Each day with him I dine.
I never get on his back,
and he never gets on mine.

The Dare

Billy Braddock swung on a swing
nearly every single day.
"I'm never, ever gonna stop swinging!"
is what he'd always say.

"I dare you to swing totally over the top!"
last week yelled Taylor Blunn.
Well, Billy did that once—
now his swinging days are done.

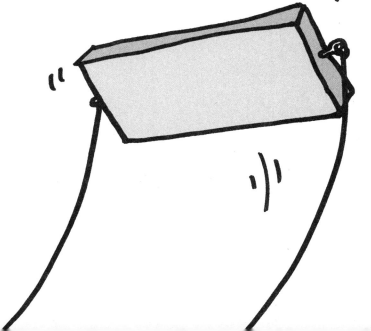

Poor Sammy Kaye

I feel sorry
for Sammy Kaye.
Earlier this very day,
he got a report card
with straight A's.

He'd better be careful
not to fall or trip
or tumble, slide, or slip
because A's are very sharp,
especially at the tip.

I am so much luckier,
I got mostly B's
except for all the C's,
grades that are round and squishy
just like boiled peas.

So, you see why I feel sorry
for that boy, Sammy Kaye,
because later on today
the poor kid's gotta walk home
with very sharp straight A's.

If I Ever Met a Caveman

If I ever met a caveman,
I'd get him clothes made of 100% cotton
because wearing woolly mammoth
must be really rotten.

Corn on the Cob

I was eating corn on the cob;
I got some in my hair.
My sister said, "How gross, you hog!"
I said, "Stick it in your ear!"

A few pieces went flying
up my brother's giant nose.
He said, "What a colossal swine you are!"
I said, "Go suck your toes!"

My mom said, "You are a pig-pig-piggy!"
as the kernels bounced *boink boink boink.*
She yelled, "Look! You've turned into one!"
All I could say was, "Oink!"

Catfish Are One Thing But . . .

Have you ever seen a fishcat?
Well, you really oughta.
It's the only fish I ever saw
that is afraid of water.

Halloween Logic

Next Halloween,

I'll be you

and you be me,

and everything will work out dandy.

Because you'll be me

and I'll be you,

and you always get more candy.

Free
Advice

If you're playing
hide-and-seek,
I suggest you hide
where folks don't look.
A very good place
that I have found
is behind this poem
inside this book.

The 4 Most Important Things You Can Do to Keep Warm When You Go Outdoors

Put on a pair of extra-thick socks;
make sure you are well fed.
Don't forget the really itchy sweater,
and wear a baboon upon your head.

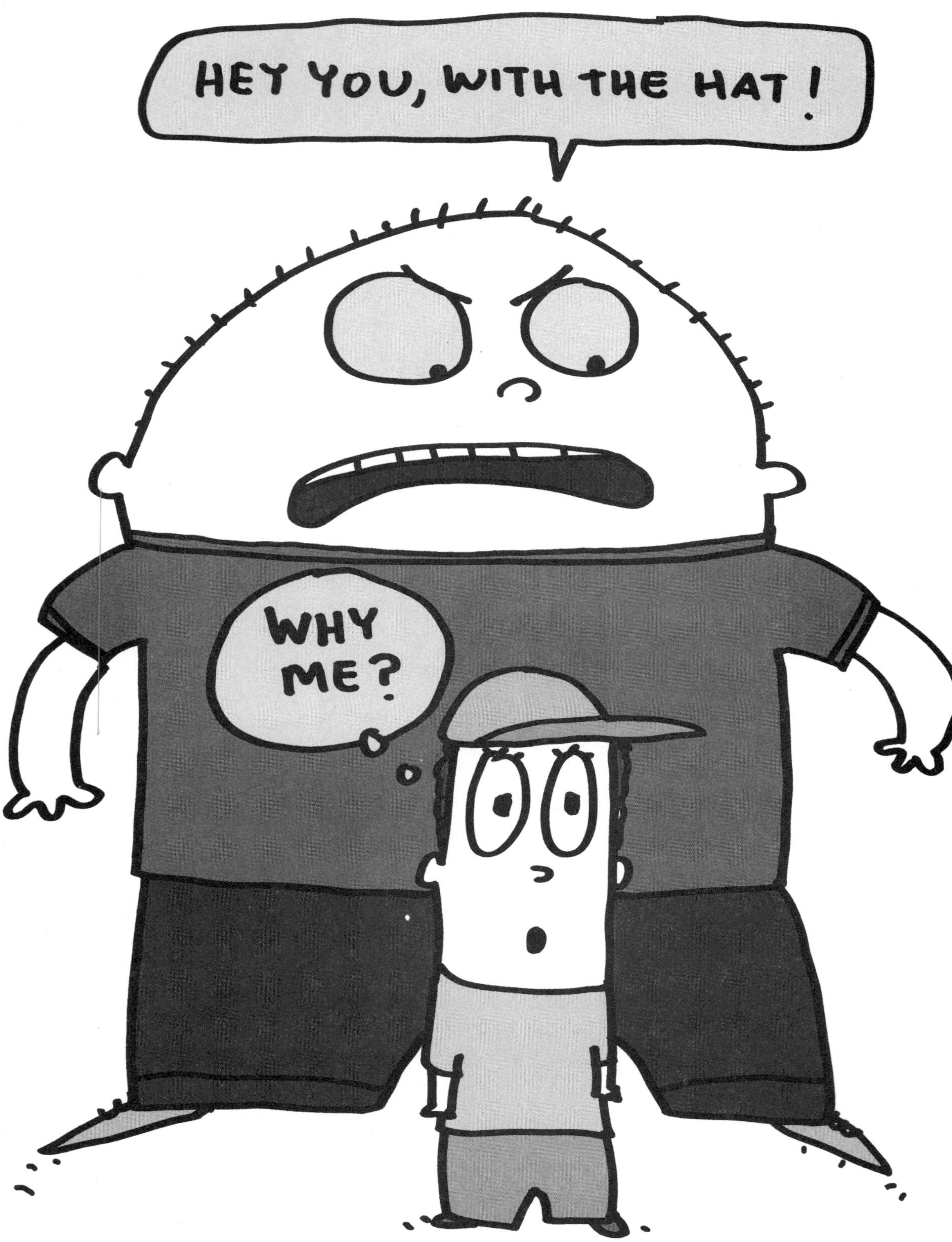
HEY YOU, WITH THE HAT!
WHY ME?

Milton, the Bully

Milton was a bully.
Milton was a rat.
Milton was a meanie.
Milton was a brat.

He picked on me at school
in every imaginable way.
I swore when I was older
I'd get revenge one day.

Now I'm a happy grown-up,
a successful maker of signs.
People come from miles around
to purchase my designs.

Yesterday, quite by chance,
Milton walked into my store.
My first instinct was to pound him
and kick him out the door.

But I am so much wiser now,
and he seemed to grow up fine.
We talked about our families
and put the past behind.

He gave me a hug before he left
and I gave his back a pat,
and yeah I stuck a sign there—
what's so wrong with that?

Why Would Anyone Ever Get Chummy With a Bug?

I never met a spydur I liked,
an antz best pal I ain't.
If I ever saw a katapillow,
I'd moore than likely faint.

The thing is I can't spelll,
so what I have to sea
is if I can make frenz
with a spellling bee.

My Cat

Why is my cat so wheezy?
Why is she constantly sneezy?
There's a very good explanation for that.
My cat
is allergic,
so very allergic,
my cat is allergic
to cats.

You're Invited

I'm terribly in love with my computer.
I may propose today,
and with any luck at all
we'll be married sometime in May.

We'll honeymoon in Paris.
What a romantic scene.
She'll stare into my eyes.
I'll stare into her screen.

Soon we'll have a family.
A boy? A girl? Who knows?
Will our baby have 126 RAM?
Will our baby have ten toes?

(sigh)

All I know is, I'm in love with my computer.
And I may propose today,
and with any luck at all
we'll be married sometime in May.

My Delightful Derriere

I'm so proud of my butt,
my roundish rump,
my delightful derriere.

My nifty bottom,
my poofy seat,
my completely wonderful rear.

(Blinkity blink)

Yours just can't compare
so don't give it a try
because your behind is human
and mine is firefly.

(Blinkity blink)

To My Mom

When my mom climbed on our television set
to vacuum a cobweb way up high,
she was the best thing I ever saw on TV,
of this I do not lie.

Professional Tree Climber, Pay Negotiable

I climb trees.
I do it very well.
I've done it a billion times,
and I've barely ever fell.

I do it all for free.
I do it all for fun.
But if you want to pay a tree climber,
then, Mister, I'm the one.

Clown College

Is there homework in clown college?
Can you get in with tiny feet?
Do you have to have a big red nose
and a knack for falling on your seat?

Must you have a flower
that squirts water in the air?
Do you need to study hard
to hold up big underwear?

Are there tests for being silly?
Are there quizzes on throwing pies?
Do you get A's for being goofy
and F's for being wise?

I want to go to such a college.
Tell me, can one be found?
Because I'd probably be an honor student
if I got grades for clownin' 'round.

My Dad Snores

Have you heard,
my dad snores so loud
it's been eight years since I've rested?
And if you haven't heard,
well then, my friend,
get those poor ears tested.

Sally Snookers, Sourpuss

Sally Snookers may be a sourpuss,
but the same could happen to you
if you also suck on a lemon
'cause your brother dares you to.

That Brother of Mine

My brother is a dirty snake!

You should see him fight.

First, he sticks his snakey tongue at me,

then he squeezes me real tight.

He's always slithering 'round the house,

dripping evil snakey goo!

Who knows just when he'll pounce on me?

He should be in a zoo!

Yeah, the boy's a snake, all right!

Of course,

I am one, too.

Babies Are Weird

Our baby is all pink
and mushy,
from its giant head
to its tiny tushie.
It doesn't even have
no hair,
it can't sit up straight
in a grown-up chair.
It's good
at spitting up lots of goo,
and its diapers are often
filled with poo.
It rubs its food
all over its face,
its language comes
from outer space.

But . . .
yesterday, it smiled at me
when it saw me pass,
as if to say "I love you,"
or maybe it had gas.

The First Time I Ever Tied My Shoes

I tied my shoes today!

I have to run and tell my mother!

Aaaaaaaagh, I fell flat on my face!

I tied them to each other!

There Is No We as We as We

You are king of your world.
You make a very nice you.
No one else on the planet
is fit to do the thing you do.

Your smile is only yours.
Your toes wiggle their own way.
The things that come out of your mouth
sound like something you would say.

You have your very own magic.
It's not at all like mine.
I have lots of shimmer.
You have all the shine.

As much as you are you
and as much as I am me,
there is no we as we as we.
And that makes me happy as can be.

My Dad Is Sort of Older Than My Grandpa

I like Grandpa.
He knows how to have fun.
I think he got so old
that he started turning young.

May I elbow you in the belly?
May I politely smack your nose?
May I kinda twist your arm?
May I pinch your precious toes?

May I rearrange your face a bit,
or at least tweak your outer ear?
May I make your funny bone go funny?
May I clobber you, my dear?

Hey, I'm a believer in nonviolence,
but this must be simply put,
I'll have to knock you silly
if you don't get off my foot!

The Peace Process

A Bit of Unpleasantness

If you ever see a real-life cow,

do not look upon its udder.

And if you do, try to forget

it's filled with stuff that makes your butter.

Shoobie doobie
ha cha cha
hee hee hee
sis boom bah

Bump bumpily bump
a scat scat doodle
flappily flap
new new noodle

Wadda wadda
bitty bitty boop
ding dong diggy
shoop shoop shoop

Nip nip nip
zonka zonka zee
tiddle tiddle tiddle
fi fo fee

Cruncha cruncha
ratty tat tat
hubba hubba hubba
zitty zitty zat

Yap yap yeah
ticky ticky toe
school is closed
because of snow!

Happy Song

I Want to Go to the Moon

I want to go to the moon,
I'd like to go there soon.

Do you know someone who's going?

I'm told there are no bees,
that the rocks taste just like cheese.

And that it's lovely there when it's glowing.

I'd appreciate its lack of alligators,
would love to skateboard down all its craters.

Plus the light air can only help my throwing.

So, I want to go to the moon,
and I'd like to go there very soon.

Do you know anyone who's going?

I must get off this planet fast.
You see, I'm the one who cuts the grass.

And my dad just noticed it needs mowing.

Hmmmm

When I grow up,
what do I want to be?
Hmmmm,
let me see.
A floor waxer?
A fax faxer?
A button maker?
A saltshaker?
A plane flier?
A clothes dryer?
A potato masher?
A garbage trasher?
A goat trainer?
A professional complainer?
(That's what my daddy is.)
Hmmmm,
when I grow up, what do I want to be?
I got it!
Six foot three!

Sing a Crazy Song

Sing a crazy song,
dance a silly dance.

Laugh large
at a tiny joke,
take a
stupid chance.

Hug the
nearest person,
read *The Cat in
the Hat.*

Always ignore
the words,
"You're too big
for that."

Index of Titles

Index of First Lines

Surprise, Surprise

Surprise, surprise.
You're not through.
I just snuck in.
How do you do?

Nice to meet you.
How have you been?
If you ever get to Poemland
you really must drop in.

I must be going,
Toodleloo.
If you want another poem
the writing's up to you.